Beneath and Beyond
the Surface

.

Beneath and Beyond
the Surface

Carroll Blair

Aveon Publishing Company

ISBN: 978-1-936430-29-1

Library of Congress Control Number
2011903178

Aveon Publishing Co.
P.O. Box 380739
Cambridge, MA 02238-0739 USA

Also by Carroll Blair

{1}

Be still, and feel the
wonder of life breathing
all around you, and
within you . . .

{2}

Behold the countless suns
of the universe, but also
the infinite space that
allows them to blaze
and project their light.

{3}

In the first motion of the
universe was the seed of
all motion that has followed
and will follow till the
rest of time.

{4}

All that is seen is of a oneness, part of the same visible world coming from the realm of the invisible.

{5}

The reach of existence is
as near as the ground to
one's feet and beyond the
distance of the most
distant star.

{6}

You are a cell of Creation,
holding its story within
your being as a cell
of the body holds
the DNA of the whole
of its being.

{7}

All things are connected
in multiple ways, yet
are as different in
as many ways.

$\{8\}$

Existence is an amalgam
of infinite places, but
has no Place.

{9}

You are of a world
complete in its
incompleteness.

{10}

Life is a magnificent dance
of ebbs and flows
seen and unseen with
nothing planned, yet
nothing happening
by happenstance.

{11}

Paradox is the great riddle,
the great enigma of life,
but also the great
understanding of
the workings of life.

{12}

Every moment carries
within it past, present
and future.

{13}

To appreciate the fullness
of life's majesty, one must
(while doing so) step
away from one's life.

{14}

The universe is faceless,
which makes it ever
beautiful; boundless,
which makes it ever
powerful; covetless,
which makes it
ever noble.

$\{15\}$

Consciousness too is
something that must
ever be created.

{16}

The mind is the sum
of its occupation at
any given moment,
changing in every
moment.

{17}

To try to attach the
mind to something
is to move against
its nature.

{18}

Trying to dissect the
multi-layered dimensions
of reality with only the
aid of the senses
is like trying to capture
running water in a
glass: the water in the
glass is clear, but
no longer running.

{19}

Cause takes place in
a moment; effect
goes on forever,
transformed.

{20}

Formlessness — that
which encompasses
all forms.

{21}

The sea . . . of endless
wave and current
dynamically rich in
life and depth . . .
this, like the world
of mind and spirit.

{22}

From thought, to feeling,
back to *thought*, back
to *feeling*, to bliss,
to light . . .

{23}

Insight, revelation,
drawn from everywhere
lighting in everything
broadening the scope
of a world, growing
with subtle intensity . . .

{24}

What is emptied
yearns to be filled;
what is filled yearns
to be emptied.

.

{25}

Every breath is a
confirmation of life.

{26}

The key to life's power is
that it is forever fresh,
forever bringing the
never existed moment
into being.

{27}

Space and Time . . .
the screen and
projector
of Eternity.

{28}

You are part of all
that happens in any
moment, because
all that happens
(and you) are part
of the infinite whole.

{29}

One separates entities to
get a closer look at them
or analyze them more
directly, but in truth
nothing in existence
is without relation
or connection to
something else.

{30}

When examined closely
everything appears to be
held together by its
most fragile elements.

$\{31\}$

What can be seen, can
be touched, can only
be as symbol to
a deeper truth.

{32}

Until life seems as if a
dream its reality has
not been experienced.

{33}

There is no difference
between distorted reality
and distorted illusion.

{34}

Reason alone cannot
give perfect reasons for what
is believed through reason.

{35}

Man names things, everything,
forgetting that they have
nothing to do with the
names they've been given,
save as a reference for an
identification that has
nothing to do with
their identity.

{36}

Man's impossible aim:
to impose subjective meaning
onto objective reality.

{37}

In the study of the world
the question mark of doubt
yields more dividends
than the period of certainty.

{38}

Presumed knowledge can
be sterile, or like stagnant
water, but thinking is
ever fluid, like a
flowing stream.

{39}

The open mind not only
allows for the new to
enter, but also the false
of the old to depart.

{40}

Should one not let life
fill him up before
filling his mind with
what he believes
life to be . . .

{41}

Think of all that is missed
of the new and unfamiliar
when comparing it
to the familiar . . .

{42}

Many things are as they
are for reasons beyond
the power of reason
to fathom.

{43}

The gift of wisdom is
the capacity to learn
from everything.

{44}

There is an awareness
and intelligence that lies
beyond the rational.

{45}

Nothing of life will ever
move an inch to
accommodate the frame
of any false picture that
man may have of it.

{46}

Life is always just
where it belongs.

{47}

Life is a self-creating,
self-sustaining force.

{48}

Death and Life are
equal in their power
to awe: one in its
finality, the other,
its infinity.

{49}

The shadows of what is
to come are all around
you, but are as invisible
as the shadows of the wind.

{50}

To go back to your beginning
you would have to journey
past your birth, all the
way back to the
Beginning.

{51}

All that you've experienced
[*all of it*] was necessary to
where you are now going.

$\{52\}$

The prints of history
lay upon the future.

{53}

There is nothing calculating
about life, but without
calculation life would
seem impossible.

{54}

Everything holds a piece
to the puzzle of existence.

{55}

To truly connect with
anything one must be
willing to take its essence
into one's being.

{56}

The greatest simplicities
are harder to comprehend
than the greatest complexities.

$\{57\}$

To be working in the
dark is not always to be
working blindly.

{58}

The sum of what anyone
knows cannot be known
to another.

{59}

To life there are many
truths, the ones revealed
to an individual, depending
on one's experiences and
the course they set
for one's life.

{60}

Truths may be provincial
or esoteric, but Truth is
not — it is for all, as
the light of the sun
shines for all.

{61}

No matter what man does
or what he believes, the
world continues to go round.

{62}

To see the world straight
is to see it in circles.

{63}

Tides are forever turning,
yet many ponder their
changing and not the
nature of the change.

{64}

Living may be put on
hold, but never life.

{65}

Everything at its time,
and in its way . . .

{66}

The clock was ticking
before the clock
was invented.

$\{67\}$

The future arrives before
you have finished
speaking its name.

{68}

Life is a cause whose
full effect can never
be known.

{69}

To engage in life is
in itself an act of faith.

{70}

Does not your past
seem like a dream? And
will not the day you are
now experiencing seem
like a dream tomorrow . . .

$\{71\}$

All relate to a world that
for no one is the same.

{72}

Much is going on as
you do what you do,
as you continue
to go on.

{73}

There are pictures
of your life around
you, without you
in the picture.

{74}

To see everything,
all must fall away.

{75}

To accept what life is
is to also accept
what it is not.

{76}

Many things can be
learned by the unlearning
of many things.

$\{77\}$

Can the world ever
add up for you
if others do
the calculations . . .

{78}

Nothing is understood until
it has made its way
into the blood of
one's understanding.

{79}

Some errors block the
way to truth; others
lead to it.

{80}

The hints that many are
most insensitive to
are the hints that
life is forever giving.

{81}

Life reveals its clues
to those who are
quiet enough to
receive them.

{82}

Wisdom begins with silence.

{83}

To wake to awareness
is to wake from the
noise that has kept
one asleep.

{84}

If silence did not exist
what quality of thought
could there be . . . (what
quality of life . . .)

{85}

As sunlight to an eclipse
is knowledge before wisdom.

{86}

The quieter the mind the
more beautiful its music.

{87}

Life's sentience finds
expression through the
human mind and spirit.

{88}

Passioned to calm . . .
there the flowers
begin to grow.

{89}

The profound wanders
all about, but silence
is its home.

{90}

It requires great space
to hold and release
great love, great bliss.

{91}

There is nothing beyond
that which is beyond words.

{92}

When one can no longer
speak one no longer
needs to.

{93}

In the realm of the spiritual
stillness can be achieved
in the midst of motion.

{94}

One of a deep spiritual nature
can be moved to the very
core of his or her being
without moving from the
center of their being.

{95}

To be *in the moment* is to
be as consumed with it
as time's consumption
of the moment.

{96}

One can witness the profound,
but one cannot experience
it until (unless) one has
been to the depths from
which it has come.

{97}

Beyond cleverness are the
quiet depths of wisdom.

{98}

If one's feeling doesn't lead
to deep thought, what can
its value be . . . if one's
thought doesn't lead to
deep feeling, what
can its value be . . .

{99}

Within the silent calm
there is great energy
and strength.

{100}

Take everything away
from a human being
but leave creativity and
he is still, she is still
a powerful entity.

{101}

To live discerningly is to
live every day as if it
were your last, but
with the eyes as if
it were your first.

{102}

The sense of awe
is the highest sense.

{103}

If not for its mystery
life could not be appreciated
as profoundly.

{104}

One cannot own the forces
that move and sustain
one's life; one can only be
humbled by them and
strive to use them wisely.

$\{105\}$

Out of one's hands is life,
but it could always use a
hand (a spiritual hand) to
help shape the beautiful
of its story.

{106}

Wherever one is at a time
one is (for that time) the
custodian of that part
of the universe.

{107}

Better than man does
Nature know the way,
but man has the
potential to transcend
the ways of Nature.

{108}

The mind is an ocean of
consciousness consisting
of depths not even
the mind is aware of.

{109}

There is great beauty and
wisdom that the human
mind and spirit has
yet to conceive.

{110}

See what the seed of a
Redwood can produce —
and so much more
the seed of a thought.

{111}

Like a bird finding its way
home, one who yearns for
light will find the way to it,
guided by the yearning within.

{112}

Truth is always present
in the inspiration whose
nature is of the spiritual.

{113}

Pathways to the sublime
appear when they are
ready to be taken.

{114}

As a cool breeze or warm
ray of sun is to the body,
so will insight often be
to the spirit.

{115}

Fret not that something of
life has passed you by . . .
it is like a wave that is
missed — others are
approaching . . .

{116}

The soul of bliss knows
nothing of before or
after — only of now.

{117}

What engages the now
may sing the song
of the eternal.

{118}

Receiving light, embracing
light, creating light . . .

{119}

To resolve to live in every moment
with the greatest verve and
conviction of purpose possible,
yet at the same time to be
fully resigned to leave one's
life at any moment without
fear or regret . . . is there
a better state of being
than this . . .

{120}

Is it not a grand phenomenon
that *anything* exists . . .

{121}

One cannot know what life
means; one can only ponder
what it means to be alive.

{122}

Life . . . the unfinished work,
yet the ultimate work of art.

ABOUT THE AUTHOR

Carroll Blair is an author of more than twenty
books and the recipient of numerous awards.
His work has been well endorsed and com-
mendably reviewed. Among his titles cited
for distinction are *Through the Shadows*, winner
of the Pacific Book Awards, and *Quarter Notes*,
winner of the Sharp Writ Book Awards.
He is an alumnus of the Boston Conservatory
and lives in Massachusetts.

www.ingramcontent.com/pod-product-compliance
Lightning Source LLC
Chambersburg PA
CBHW020040040426
42331CB00030B/105